Easy Sandwich Cookbook

50 Amazingly Delicious Sandwich Recipes

By
BookSumo Press

Published by
http://www.booksumo.com

ENJOY THE RECIPES?

KEEP ON COOKING WITH 6 MORE FREE COOKBOOKS!

Visit our website and simply enter your email address to join the club and receive your 6 cookbooks.

http://booksumo.com/magnet

 https://www.instagram.com/booksumopress/

 https://www.facebook.com/booksumo/

LEGAL NOTES

Table of Contents

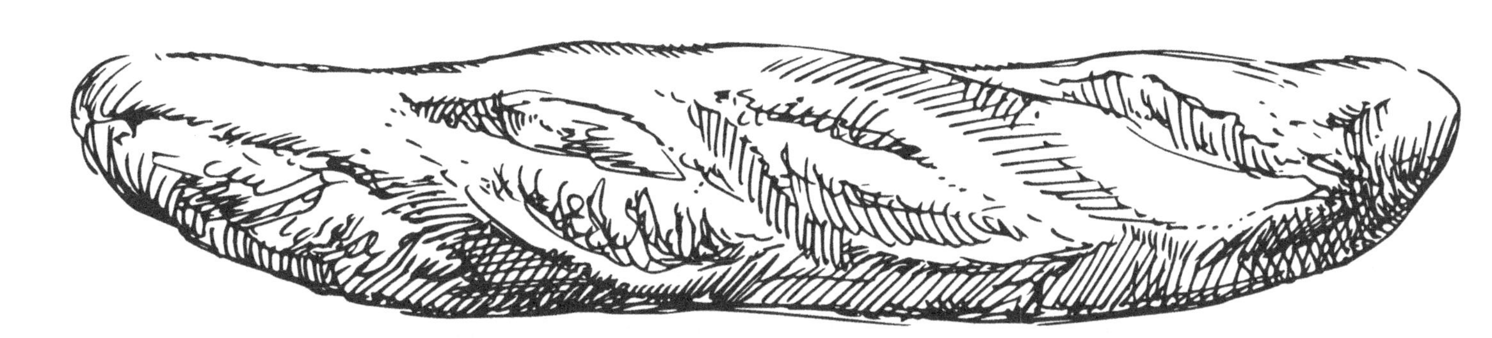

EGGPLANT, Basil, Feta Sandwich

Prep Time: 20 mins
Total Time: 30 mins

Servings per Recipe: 2	
Calories	802 kcal
Fat	39.5 g
Carbohydrates	91.3g
Protein	23.8 g
Cholesterol	44 mg
Sodium	1460 mg

Ingredients

1 small eggplant, halved and sliced
1 tbsp olive oil, or as needed
1/4 C. mayonnaise
2 cloves garlic, minced
2 (6 inch) French sandwich rolls
1 small tomato, sliced
1/2 C. crumbled feta cheese
1/4 C. minced fresh basil leaves

Directions

1. Turn on your broiler to low if possible.
2. Get a bowl, mix: garlic and mayo.
3. Take your eggplant pieces and coat them with olive oil. Put them on a sheet for baking.
4. For 10 mins cook the eggplant in the broiler 6 inches from the heat.
5. Cut your French bread in half and toast it.
6. Spread a good amount of mayo and garlic mix on your bread and layer the following to form a sandwich: tomato, basil leaves, eggplant, and feta.
7. Enjoy.

Balsamic Mushroom Sandwich

Prep Time: 8 mins
Total Time: 20 mins

Servings per Recipe: 4	
Calories	445 kcal
Fat	33.4 g
Carbohydrates	31.4g
Protein	7.8 g
Cholesterol	5 mg
Sodium	426 mg

Ingredients

2 cloves garlic, minced
6 tbsps olive oil
1/2 tsp dried thyme
2 tbsps balsamic vinegar
salt and pepper to taste
4 large Portobello mushroom caps
4 hamburger buns
1 tbsp capers
1/4 C. mayonnaise
1 tbsp capers, drained
1 large tomato, sliced
4 leaves lettuce

Directions

1. Preheat your broiler and set its rack so that it is near the heating source before doing anything else.
2. Get a bowl and mix: pepper, garlic, salt, olive oil, vinegar, and thyme.
3. Get a 2nd bowl, combine: mayo and capers.
4. Coat your mushrooms with half of the dressing.
5. Then toast the veggies for 5 mins under the broiler.
6. Flip the mushrooms after coating the opposite side with the remaining dressing.
7. Toast everything for 5 more mins.
8. Now also toast your bread.
9. Apply some mayo to the bread before layering a mushroom, some lettuce and tomato.
10. Enjoy.

MEATBALL MADNESS Sandwich

Prep Time: 20 mins
Total Time: 40 mins

Servings per Recipe: 4

Calories	781 kcal
Fat	31.9 g
Carbohydrates	78.2g
Protein	43.6 g
Cholesterol	141 mg
Sodium	1473 mg

Ingredients

1 lb ground beef
3/4 C. bread crumbs
2 tsps dried Italian seasoning
2 cloves garlic, minced
2 tbsps minced fresh parsley
2 tbsps grated Parmesan cheese
1 egg, beaten
1 French baguette
1 tbsp extra-virgin olive oil
1/2 tsp garlic powder
1 pinch salt, or to taste
1 (14 oz.) jar spaghetti sauce
4 slices provolone cheese

Directions

1. Set your oven to 350 degrees before doing anything else.
2. Get a bowl, combine: eggs, beef, parmesan, bread crumbs, parsley, garlic, and Italian seasoning.
3. Mold the mix into your preferred size of meatballs and cook them in the oven for 22 mins.
4. Now cut your bread and take out some of the inside so the meatballs fit better.
5. Toast the bread for 6 mins in the oven after coating it with some olive oil, salt, and garlic powder.
6. Get a saucepan and heat up your pasta sauce.
7. Add in your meatballs to the sauce after they are cooked and mix everything.
8. Put some meatballs into your bread and then toast the sandwich in the oven for 4 mins before serving.
9. Enjoy.

The Spring Time Sandwich

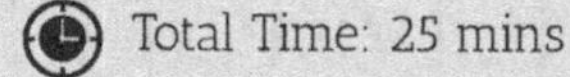

Prep Time: 25 mins
Total Time: 25 mins

Servings per Recipe: 4	
Calories	811 kcal
Fat	56.1 g
Carbohydrates	29.6g
Protein	46.3 g
Cholesterol	204 mg
Sodium	908 mg

Ingredients

1/2 C. mayonnaise
1/4 C. blue cheese dressing
8 slices multigrain bread
2 cooked chicken breasts, sliced
1 ripe avocado, sliced
8 slices cooked turkey bacon
2 hard-boiled eggs, minced
4 lettuce leaves

Directions

1. Get a bowl and mix the blue cheese with some mayo.
2. Coat your bread with 2 tbsps of this mix.
3. Place a quarter of your chicken breast on four pieces of bread.
4. Then layer the following on each piece: lettuce, avocado, hard-boiled egg, bacon, another piece of bread.
5. Enjoy with some blue cheese on the side for dipping.

THE FLUFFY Sandwich

Prep Time: 4 mins
Total Time: 5 mins

Servings per Recipe: 1

Calories	373 kcal
Fat	18.1 g
Carbohydrates	43.5g
Protein	12.1 g
Cholesterol	0 mg
Sodium	502 mg

Ingredients

2 tbsps peanut butter
2 slices bread
2 1/2 tbsps marshmallow cream

Directions

1. Lay two pieces of bread flat on a working surface.
2. Coat one piece of bread with peanut butter, and another piece with marshmallow cream.
3. Now microwave the pieces of bread for 30 secs with the highest power setting.
4. Form the pieces into a sandwich and enjoy with milk.

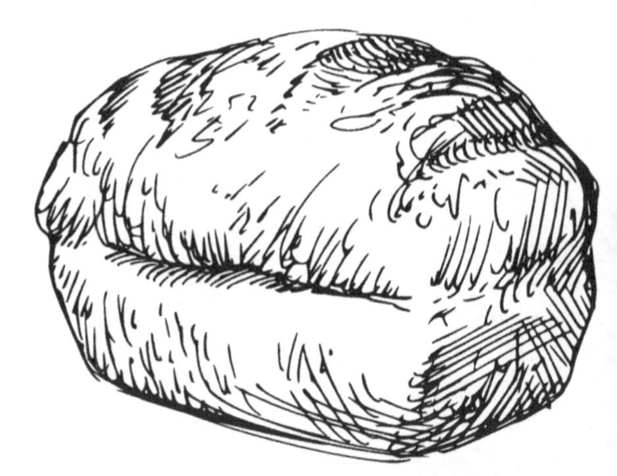

Pepperoncini Sandwich

Prep Time: 10 mins
Total Time: 10 mins

Servings per Recipe: 1	
Calories	496 kcal
Fat	32.5 g
Carbohydrates	46.3g
Protein	11.4 g
Cholesterol	32 mg
Sodium	1024 mg

Ingredients

2 thick slices whole wheat bread
2 tbsps cream cheese, softened
6 slices cucumber
2 tbsps alfalfa sprouts
1 tsp olive oil
1 tsp red wine vinegar
1 tomato, sliced
1 leaf lettuce
1 oz. pepperoncini, sliced
1/2 avocado, mashed

Directions

1. Layer one piece of bread with the following: 1 tbsp of cream cheese, alfalfa sprouts, oil and vinegar, cucumber pieces, tomatoes, pepperoncini, and lettuce.
2. Coat another piece of bread with avocado and form a sandwich.
3. Enjoy.

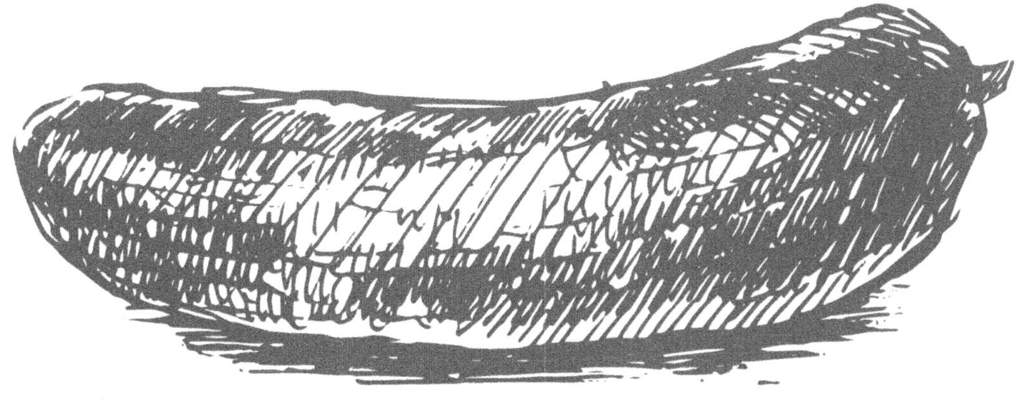

SUMMER Sandwich

Prep Time: 15 mins
Total Time: 20 mins

Servings per Recipe: 8	
Calories	386 kcal
Fat	21.5 g
Carbohydrates	31.6g
Protein	16.8 g
Cholesterol	40 mg
Sodium	738 mg

Ingredients

1 (1 lb) loaf ciabatta bread
3/4 C. pesto
8 oz. fontina cheese, sliced
2 ripe tomatoes, sliced
4 leaves butter lettuce

Directions

1. Turn on your oven's broiler to low if possible.
2. Cut your bread in half. Coat one side with some pesto then layer the following on the other side: tomato, and fontina cheese.
3. Place the pieces of bread which have cheese under the broiler until the cheese has melted.
4. Top this piece with some lettuce.
5. Form sandwiches then cut them in half for serving.
6. Enjoy.

Easy European Sandwich

Prep Time: 15 mins

Total Time: 15 mins

Servings per Recipe: 25	
Calories	233 kcal
Fat	12.9 g
Carbohydrates	21.9g
Protein	7.7 g
Cholesterol	39 mg
Sodium	470 mg

Ingredients

1 (8 oz.) package cream cheese, softened
1/2 C. butter, softened
1 tbsp minced garlic
2 loaves French bread, sliced
1 lb sliced sausage of your choice
1 cucumber, sliced
3 medium tomatoes, sliced
1 hard-cooked egg, minced

Directions

1. Get a bowl, mix: garlic, butter, and cream cheese.
2. Coat a piece of bread with this mix.
3. Then layer the following on each bread piece: tomato, sausage, cucumber, egg.
4. Enjoy this sandwich open.

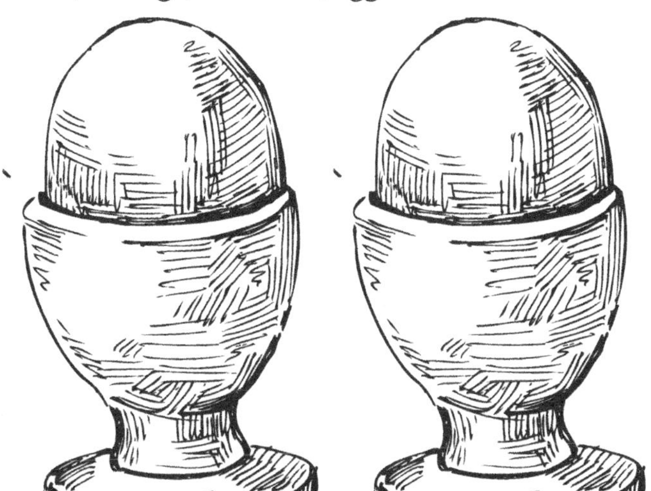

THE BROOKLYN STYLE Sandwich

Prep Time: 30 mins
Total Time: 45 mins

Servings per Recipe: 4	
Calories	892 kcal
Fat	45.3 g
Carbohydrates	79.5g
Protein	42.7 g
Cholesterol	97 mg
Sodium	1604 mg

Ingredients

3 C. shredded cabbage
2 tbsps vegetable oil
2 tbsps apple cider vinegar
2 tbsps white sugar
1 tsp adobo seasoning
1 tsp ground black pepper
4 C. vegetable oil for frying
3 whole russet potatoes
8 thick slices Italian bread
1 lb sliced pastrami (divided)
4 slices provolone cheese
8 slices tomato

Directions

1. Get a bowl and combine evenly: black pepper, cabbage, adobo, veggie oil (2 tbsps), sugar, and vinegar.
2. Get a large pot and get your oil to 375 degrees then set your oven to 225 degrees before doing anything else.
3. Dice your potatoes into slices and fry them in the oil for 6 mins.
4. Now place the potatoes to the side.
5. For 6 mins toast your bread in the oven.
6. On 4 slices of bread layer: pastrami and cheese.
7. Now toast the pieces for 4 more mins to melt the cheese.
8. Layer the following on the pastrami: 2 tomato pieces, cabbage mix, fried potatoes, and another piece of toasted bread.
9. Enjoy.

Tempeh Sandwich (Vegetarian Approved)

Prep Time: 10 mins
Total Time: 30 mins

Servings per Recipe: 4	
Calories	392 kcal
Fat	24.8 g
Carbohydrates	24.4g
Protein	21.7 g
Cholesterol	28 mg
Sodium	551 mg

Ingredients

1 tbsp sesame oil
1 (8 oz.) package tempeh, sliced into thin strips
2 tbsps liquid amino acid supplement
1 tbsp sesame oil
1 small onion, thinly sliced
1 medium green bell pepper, thinly sliced
1 jalapeno pepper, sliced
2 pita breads, cut in half
soy mayonnaise
4 thin slices Swiss cheese

Directions

1. For 5 mins fry your tempeh in hot oil, add half of the amino's liquid, then cook everything for 2 more mins.
2. Flip all the tempeh pieces and continue frying them for another 2 mins.
3. Now add the rest of the amino's liquid and cook the mix for 2 more mins.
4. Place everything to the side.
5. Stir fry your jalapenos, onions, and green peppers for 6 mins with fresh oil in the same pan.
6. Coat each piece of pita with some mayo (1 tsp).
7. Then fill each piece with some onion mix, tempeh, and Swiss cheese.
8. For 2 mins toast the pita in a toaster oven or on the stove until the Swiss melts.
9. Enjoy.

EASY EGG
and American Sandwich

Prep Time: 1 min
Total Time: 5 mins

Servings per Recipe: 1	
Calories	318 kcal
Fat	15.8 g
Carbohydrates	26.9g
Protein	16.9 g
Cholesterol	214 mg
Sodium	839 mg

Ingredients

1 egg
1 tbsp milk
2 slices white bread
salt and pepper to taste (optional)
1 slice American cheese

Directions

1. Get a bowl, and mix: whisked eggs, salt, pepper, and milk.
2. Microwave the mix for 90 secs in the microwave with the highest power setting.
3. Simultaneously toast your bread slices then add your egg to the toasted bread.
4. Before forming a sandwich top the egg with a piece of cheese.
5. Now heat everything in the microwave for 30 more secs.
6. Enjoy.

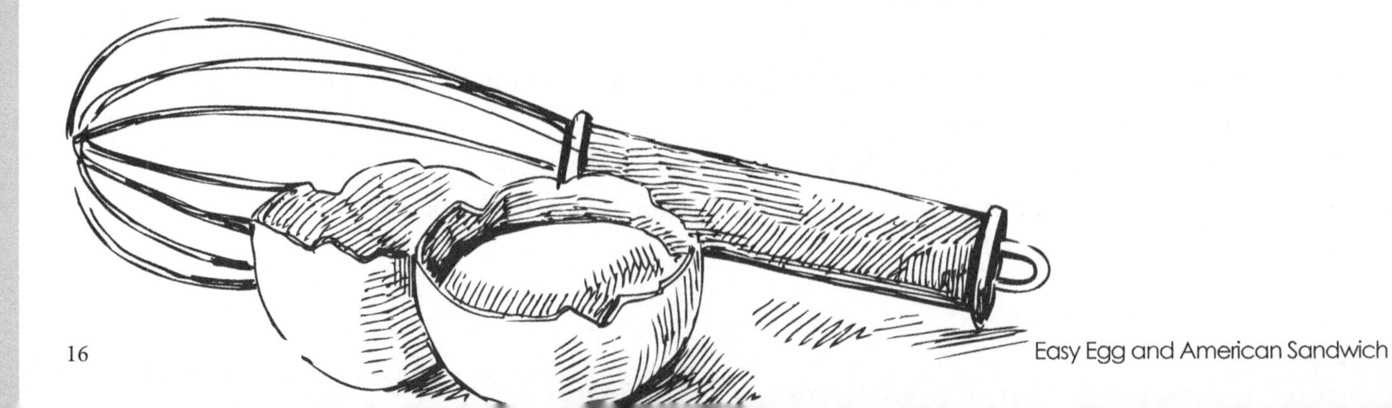

The
Moscow

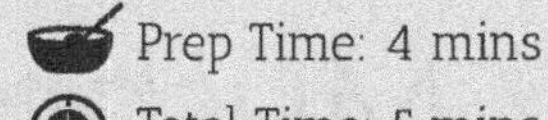 Prep Time: 4 mins

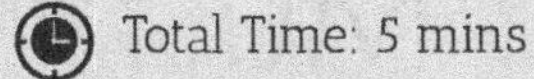 Total Time: 5 mins

Servings per Recipe: 1	
Calories	535 kcal
Fat	28.8 g
Carbohydrates	38.7g
Protein	30.8 g
Cholesterol	88 mg
Sodium	2472 mg

Ingredients

2 slices American cheese
2 slices white bread, toasted
3 slices deli-style sliced turkey breast
2 tbsps Russian salad dressing

Directions

1. On one piece of toasted bread put 1 piece of cheese.
2. Now heat it in the microwave for 30 secs.
3. Layer some turkey on the cheese and on the remaining piece of bread coat it with some Russian dressing.
4. Form a sandwich and enjoy.

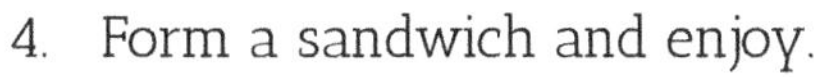

COUNTRYSIDE BEEF and Mushroom Sandwich

Prep Time: 25 mins
Total Time: 6 hrs 45 mins

Servings per Recipe: 6

Calories	516 kcal
Fat	22.3 g
Carbohydrates	42.9g
Protein	34.3 g
Cholesterol	78 mg
Sodium	635 mg

Ingredients

1 loaf hearty country bread, unsliced
3 tbsps vegetable oil, divided
1 (3 lb) boneless beef round steak, 2 inches thick
1 onion, thinly sliced
2 C. sliced fresh mushrooms
1 clove garlic, minced, or to taste
salt to taste
ground black pepper to taste
garlic salt to taste

Directions

1. Slice off a piece of bread from the loaf and keep it for later.
2. Now remove the inside center of the loaf. This space is to be filled later.
3. Fry your steak in 1 tbsp of veggie oil for 6 mins per side then place the steak to the side.
4. Stir fry your mushrooms, onions, and garlic for 7 mins until the onions are see through in 2 more tbsps of veggie oil.
5. Fill the hollowed bread with: the mushrooms, onions, and steak.
6. Put the first piece of bread you sliced off earlier back on the loaf.
7. Now cover everything with foil.
8. Lay the bread in a casserole dish and place something heavy on top of it. Like a cast iron frying pan with jars of water in it.
9. For 7 hrs let the bread sit in the fridge with the pan on top of it.
10. When ready to serve, cut the sandwich into servings.
11. Enjoy.

Fruity Neufchatel Sandwich

Prep Time: 15 mins
Total Time: 15 mins

Servings per Recipe: 8	
Calories	289 kcal
Fat	10.3 g
Carbohydrates	40.4g
Protein	10.6 g
Cholesterol	21 mg
Sodium	344 mg

Ingredients

1 (8 oz.) package Neufchatel cheese, softened
1/4 C. crushed pineapple, drained
4 bananas, sliced
1/2 C. shredded coconut
16 slices whole-grain bread

Directions

1. Get a bowl, mix: pineapple and cheese.
2. Coat one piece of bread with this mix and then layer some banana on top of it, top everything with a final layer of coconut.
3. Form a sandwich with another piece of bread.
4. Enjoy.

THE LITTLE TIKE
Sandwich

Prep Time: 10 mins
Total Time: 10 mins

Servings per Recipe: 3	
Calories	250 kcal
Fat	15.8 g
Carbohydrates	21.4g
Protein	8.5 g
Cholesterol	0 mg
Sodium	104 mg

Ingredients

1/4 C. peanut butter, or to taste
1 Gala apple, cored and sliced horizontally into discs
1/2 C. granola

Directions

1. Apply a coating of peanut butter to each piece of apple. Then top everything with some granola.
2. Lay two pieces of apples together, joining them at the granola and peanut butter.
3. Repeat with the remaining apple pieces to form apple sandwiches.
4. Enjoy.

Bacon Hawaiian Sandwich

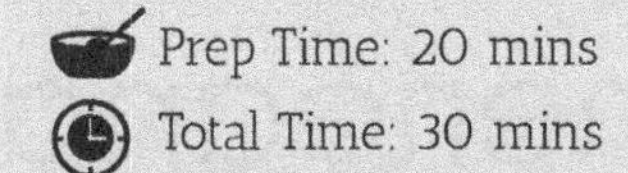

Prep Time: 20 mins
Total Time: 30 mins

Servings per Recipe: 8	
Calories	491 kcal
Fat	35.4 g
Carbohydrates	27.1g
Protein	15.5 g
Cholesterol	68 mg
Sodium	819 mg

Ingredients

16 turkey slices turkey bacon
8 slices toasted white bread
1 (20 oz.) can sliced pineapple, drained
8 slices Cheddar cheese

Directions

1. Fry your bacon until crispy then remove any excess oils.
2. Layer your bread in a broiler pan or on a baking sheet.
3. Top the bread with some pineapple, bacon, and cheese.
4. Now broil everything for a few mins until it is bubbly.
5. Form 4 sandwiches from the toasted bread.
6. Enjoy.

THE Americana

Prep Time: 5 mins
Total Time: 10 mins

Servings per Recipe: 1	
Calories	488 kcal
Fat	32.1 g
Carbohydrates	29.2g
Protein	21.3 g
Cholesterol	91 mg
Sodium	1081 mg

Ingredients

2 slices sourdough bread
1 tbsp butter
1 tbsp grated Parmesan cheese
1 slice American cheese
1 slice Cheddar cheese

Directions

1. Coat a single side of each piece of bread with some butter. Then add some parmesan to this side and place it downwards in a frying pan.
2. Now place a piece of American and cheddar cheese on top of the bread.
3. Add another piece of bread on top of the cheese with its buttered side facing upwards to form a sandwich.
4. Fry the sandwich for a few mins until it is golden on both sides.
5. Enjoy.

Rustic Beef Sandwich

Prep Time: 40 mins
Total Time: 45 mins

Servings per Recipe: 8

Calories	493 kcal
Fat	29.8 g
Carbohydrates	35.4g
Protein	21 g
Cholesterol	84 mg
Sodium	754 mg

Ingredients

1 (1 lb) loaf French or Italian-style bread
1/4 C. minced green onions
1 tbsp milk
1/8 tsp garlic powder
1 green bell pepper, sliced in rings
1 lb ground beef
1 C. sour cream
1 tsp Worcestershire sauce
3/4 tsp salt
2 tbsps butter, softened
2 tomatoes, sliced
1 C. shredded Cheddar cheese

Directions

1. Divide your bread in half, cover it in foil, and place it in the oven at 375 degrees for 13 mins.
2. Fry your beef and onions and remove any excess oils.
3. Now add in the following to the mix: pepper, milk, salt, garlic, Worcestershire, garlic, and sour cream.
4. Heat this mixture for 2 mins.
5. Coat your bread with butter, then layer the following: half of your beef mix, bell peppers, tomatoes and cheese.
6. Cook everything in the oven for 6 mins at 350 degrees.
7. Form a sandwich and enjoy.

CORNED BEEF and Sauerkraut Sandwich

Prep Time: 15 mins
Total Time: 45 mins

Servings per Recipe: 4

Calories	657 kcal
Fat	40.3 g
Carbohydrates	43.5g
Protein	32.1 g
Cholesterol	115 mg
Sodium	1930 mg

Ingredients

2 tbsps butter
8 slices rye bread
8 slices deli sliced corned beef
8 slices Swiss cheese
1 C. sauerkraut, drained
1/2 C. Thousand Island dressing

Directions

1. Coat one side of your bread with butter. Then coat the opposite side with dressing.
2. Place the following on four pieces of bread: 1 piece of Swiss, one fourth C. sauerkraut, 2 pieces of corned beef, the rest of the Swiss.
3. Add another piece of bread and make sure the buttered sides are facing outwards.
4. Fry the sandwiches for 15 mins on each side.
5. Enjoy.

Roast Beef and Provolone Sandwich

Prep Time: 5 mins
Total Time: 15 mins

Servings per Recipe: 4	
Calories	548 kcal
Fat	22.6 g
Carbohydrates	40.5g
Protein	44.6 g
Cholesterol	94 mg
Sodium	2310 mg

Ingredients

1 (10.5 oz.) can beef consommé
1 C. water
1 lb thinly sliced deli roast beef
8 slices provolone cheese
4 hoagie rolls, split lengthwise

Directions

1. Set your oven to 350 degrees before doing anything else.
2. Open your rolls and place them in a casserole dish.
3. Now combine water and beef consommé in a pan to make a broth.
4. Cook your beef in this mixture for 5 mins.
5. Then divide the meat between your rolls and top them with cheese.
6. Cook the rolls in the oven for 6 mins.
7. Enjoy the sandwiches dipped in broth..

OREGANO Mozzarella Sandwich

Prep Time: 8 mins
Total Time: 15 mins

Servings per Recipe: 6

Calories	394 kcal
Fat	18.3 g
Carbohydrates	42g
Protein	15 g
Cholesterol	46 mg
Sodium	1032 mg

Ingredients

1/4 C. unsalted butter
1/8 tsp garlic powder (optional)
12 slices white bread
1 tsp dried oregano
1 (8 oz.) package shredded mozzarella cheese
1 (24 oz.) jar vodka marinara sauce

Directions

1. Turn on the broiler before doing anything else.
2. Get a baking dish and lay half of your bread pieces in it.
3. On top of each piece of bread put some mozzarella. Then top the cheese with the remaining pieces of bread.
4. With a butter knife coat each sandwich with some butter. Then season the butter by applying some oregano and garlic powder.
5. Broil the sandwiches for 4 mins then flip it and apply more butter, oregano, and garlic to its opposite side.
6. Continue broiling the sandwich for another 4 mins.
7. Enjoy with the marinara as a dip.

Toasted Cinnamon Sandwich

Prep Time: 5 mins
Total Time: 10 mins

Servings per Recipe: 1	
Calories	469 kcal
Fat	26.6 g
Carbohydrates	37.3g
Protein	20 g
Cholesterol	80 mg
Sodium	907 mg

Ingredients

2 links beef sausage links
1 slice Cheddar cheese
2 frozen waffles, toasted
1/4 Red Delicious apple, sliced very thin
1/2 tsp cinnamon-sugar

Directions

1. Stir fry your sausage for 6 mins until it is fully done.
2. Lay one piece of cheese on a waffle then place your apples on top of the cheese.
3. Top the apples with the cinnamon-sugar and the sausage.
4. Place the apples over the waffles and slice the sandwich in half.
5. Enjoy.

SOCAL Sandwich (Vegetarian Approved)

Prep Time: 30 mins
Total Time: 50 mins

Servings per Recipe: 4

Calories	393 kcal
Fat	23.8 g
Carbohydrates	36.5g
Protein	9.2 g
Cholesterol	22 mg
Sodium	623 mg

Ingredients

1/4 C. mayonnaise
3 cloves garlic, minced
1 tbsp lemon juice
1/8 C. olive oil
1 C. sliced red bell peppers
1 small zucchini, sliced
1 red onion, sliced
1 small yellow squash, sliced
2 (4-x6-inch) focaccia bread pieces, split horizontally
1/2 C. crumbled feta cheese

Directions

1. Get a bowl, combine: lemon juice, mayo, and minced garlic.
2. Place a covering of plastic on the bowl and put everything in the fridge.
3. Now get your outdoor grill hot and coat the grate with oil.
4. Lay your zucchini and bell peppers in the center of the grate then spread the squash and onions around the peppers.
5. Grill the veggies for 5 mins then flip them and continue grilling for 4 more mins.
6. Now remove everything from the grill.
7. Coat your pieces of bread with the mayo mix liberally then add some feta to each.
8. Lay your bread on the grill with the cheese facing upwards and toast the bottoms of the bread for 4 mins.
9. Top the sandwiches evenly with the veggies and serve open faced.
10. Enjoy.

Honey Bread for Sandwiches

Prep Time: 30 mins
Total Time: 2 hrs 45 mins

Servings per Recipe: 14	
Calories	191 kcal
Fat	4.7 g
Carbohydrates	31.9g
Protein	5.8 g
Cholesterol	24 mg
Sodium	163 mg

Ingredients

1 1/4 C. warm milk
1 egg, beaten
2 tbsps butter, softened
1/4 C. honey
3/4 tsp salt
2 3/4 C. bread flour
1 C. whole wheat flour
1 1/4 tsps bread machine yeast
2 tbsps butter, melted

Directions

1. Add all the ingredients to a bread machine and set the machine to the dough cycle.
2. Now roll the bread into a thickness of 1 inch and slice the dough into rolls with a biscuit or cookie cutter.
3. Layer the rolls in a jellyroll pan that has been coated with nonstick spray and place a kitchen towel over everything.
4. Let the dough sit for 65 mins. After 35 mins set your oven to 350 degrees before continuing.
5. Once the dough has sat for 65 mins and the oven is hot cook the rolls in the oven for 12 mins then top them with some melted butter liberally.
6. Enjoy.

THE BEST

Egg Salad Sandwich

Prep Time: 10 mins
Total Time: 35 mins

Servings per Recipe: 4

Calories	344 kcal
Fat	31.9 g
Carbohydrates	2.3g
Protein	< 13 g
Cholesterol	382 mg
Sodium	1351 mg

Ingredients

8 eggs
1/2 C. mayonnaise
1 tsp prepared yellow mustard
1/4 C. chopped green onion
salt and pepper to taste
1/4 tsp paprika

Directions

1. Get your eggs boiling in water.
2. Once the water is boiling, shut the heat, place a lid on the pot, and let the eggs sit in the water for 15 mins.
3. Drain the liquid, remove the shells, and dice the eggs.
4. Now grab a bowl, combine: green onions, eggs, mustard, and mayo.
5. Stir the mix until it is smooth and even then top everything with the paprika, some pepper, and salt.
6. Stir the mix again then serve the salad on some warmed bread rolls.
7. Enjoy.

Pesto Provolone American Sandwich

Prep Time: 5 mins
Total Time: 15 mins

Servings per Recipe: 1	
Calories	503 kcal
Fat	36.5 g
Carbohydrates	24.2g
Protein	20.4 g
Cholesterol	82 mg
Sodium	1108 mg

Ingredients

2 slices Italian bread
1 tbsp softened butter, divided
1 tbsp prepared pesto sauce, divided
1 slice provolone cheese
2 slices tomato
1 slice American cheese

Directions

1. Coat a piece of bread with butter and place the bread in a frying pan with the buttered side facing downwards.
2. Top the bread with 1/2 of the pesto sauce, some tomato, 1 piece of provolone, and 1 piece of American.
3. Grab the other piece of bread and coat it with the rest of the pesto and place the pesto side of the bread on top of the cheese.
4. Coat the top of the bread with more butter and cook the sandwich for 6 mins each side.
5. Enjoy.

VODKA SAUCE Sandwich

Prep Time: 8 mins
Total Time: 15 mins

Servings per Recipe: 6

Calories	394 kcal
Fat	18.3 g
Carbohydrates	42g
Protein	15 g
Cholesterol	46 mg
Sodium	1032 mg

Ingredients

1/4 C. unsalted butter
1/8 tsp garlic powder
12 slices white bread
1 tsp dried oregano
1 (8 oz.) package shredded mozzarella cheese
1 (24 oz.) jar vodka marinara sauce

Directions

1. Get your oven's broiler hot before doing anything else.
2. Grab a jelly roll pan and layer 6 pieces of bread in it.
3. Top the bread evenly with some mozzarella then place the remaining bread pieces.
4. Get a bowl, combine: garlic powder and butter.
5. Top the sandwiches with 1 tbsp of the butter mix. Then coat everything with some oregano.
6. Broil the sandwiches for 3 mins then turn the sandwiches over and coat the bread with another tbsp of butter and more oregano.
7. Continue broiling for 3 more mins then divide the sandwiches into 2 pieces.
8. Enjoy dipped in the marinara sauce.

Onion Bread for Sandwiches

Prep Time: 3 hrs 20 mins
Total Time: 3 hrs 20 mins

Servings per Recipe: 8	
Calories	260 kcal
Fat	5.3 g
Carbohydrates	45.9g
Protein	6.9 g
Cholesterol	13 mg
Sodium	487 mg

Ingredients

3/4 C. lukewarm milk
5 tbsps lukewarm water
3 tbsps butter, softened
1 1/2 tsps salt
3 tbsps white sugar
1 tsp onion powder
3 tbsps dried minced onion
1/4 C. instant potato flakes
3 C. all-purpose flour
1 (.25 oz.) envelope active dry yeast
1 egg white
1 tbsp water
1/4 C. dried minced onion

Directions

1. Add the following to a bread machine and set the machine to the dough cycle: yeast, milk, flour, water, potato flakes, butter, 3 tbsps of dried onions, salt, onion powder, and sugar.
2. Now work the dough on a cutting board coated with flour for 2 mins then slice the dough into 8 pieces. Shape each piece into a ball then flatten each one.
3. Place the flattened dough in a jellyroll pan which has been coated with nonstick spray and place a kitchen towel over everything.
4. Let the dough sit for 50 mins. Now set your oven to 350 degrees before doing anything else.
5. Get a small bowl and whisk your water and egg together. Top the rolls with the egg wash then coat each one with the rest of the minced onions.
6. Cook everything in the oven for 17 mins.
7. Enjoy.

THE Reuben

Prep Time: 10 mins
Total Time: 20 mins

Servings per Recipe: 2	
Calories	760 kcal
Fat	43.9 g
Carbohydrates	48.9g
Protein	44.7 g
Cholesterol	150 mg
Sodium	3088 mg

Ingredients

1 C. sauerkraut, drained
10 oz. sliced deli turkey meat
2 tbsps butter
4 slices marble rye bread
4 slices Swiss cheese
4 tbsps thousand island salad dressing, or to taste

Directions

1. Place the following in a bowl: turkey, and sauerkraut.
2. Place the mix in the microwave for 1 mins.
3. Now coat one side of each piece of bread with butter liberally then coat the other piece with some dressing.
4. Evenly distribute your Swiss, sauerkraut, and turkey on two pieces of bread.
5. Top the meat with the other piece of bread with its buttered side facing upwards.
6. Now fry your sandwiches with the buttered side facing downwards for 8 mins, flipping the sandwich halfway.
7. Enjoy.

Cranberry Curry Sandwich

Prep Time: 20 mins
Total Time: 20 mins

Servings per Recipe: 6

Calories	528 kcal
Fat	32.7 g
Carbohydrates	43.9g
Protein	16.5 g
Cholesterol	47 mg
Sodium	540 mg

Ingredients

2 C. cubed, cooked chicken
1 unpeeled red apple, chopped
3/4 C. dried cranberries
1/2 C. thinly sliced celery
1/4 C. chopped pecans
2 tbsps thinly sliced green onions
3/4 C. mayonnaise
2 tsps lime juice
1/2 tsp curry powder
12 slices bread
12 lettuce leaves

Directions

1. Get a bowl, combine: green onions, chicken, pecans, apple, celery, and cranberries.
2. Stir the mix then add in the curry, lime juice, and mayo.
3. Stir the mix again to working in the spices.
4. Place a covering of plastic on the bowl and put everything in the fridge until chilled.
5. Slice the crust off of the pieces of bread and liberally divide the chicken mix between half of the slices then top the mix with 1 piece of lettuce and layer the remaining pieces of bread to form a sandwich.
6. Enjoy.

THE ATHENIAN DREAM Sandwich

Prep Time: 30 mins
Total Time: 45 mins

Servings per Recipe: 8	
Calories	681 kcal
Fat	36.4 g
Carbohydrates	44.9g
Protein	43.7 g
Cholesterol	108 mg
Sodium	1087 mg

Ingredients

Artichoke Aioli:
1 (6.5 oz.) jar marinated artichoke hearts, drained
2 tbsps mayonnaise
2 tbsps grated Parmesan cheese
1 tsp lemon zest
1/2 lemon, juiced
1/4 tsp red pepper flakes
salt and ground black pepper to taste
Filling:
2 tbsps olive oil
1 1/2 lbs beef tri-tip steak, thinly sliced
1 tsp Italian seasoning
1 onion, sliced thin
1 yellow bell pepper, sliced into strips
1 orange bell pepper, sliced into strips
1/4 C. pickled sweet and hot pepper rings
1/4 C. garlic basil spread (see footnote for recipe link)
1 C. sliced mushrooms
1 tbsp capers
1 tbsp Marsala wine
1 anchovy fillet (optional)
12 slices aged provolone cheese
1/4 C. crumbled Gorgonzola cheese

Directions

1. Puree the following with a food processor: black pepper, artichoke, salt, mayo, pepper flakes, parmesan, lemon juice, and lemon zest.
2. Add the mix to a bowl and place a covering of plastic over the bowl.
3. Put everything in the fridge.
4. Begin to stir fry your steak, in a saucepan, in olive oil, for 5 mins then top the meat with some black pepper, salt, and the Italian spice.

5. Stir the spice into the meat then combine in: garlic basil spread, onions, sweet hot pepper, yellow pepper, and orange pepper.
6. Stir the mix and cook everything for 7 mins then combine in: the anchovy, mushrooms, Marsala, and capers.
7. Let the mix cook for 6 more mins.
8. Add in your cheese and let it melt (2 to 4 more mins of heating).
9. Now shut the heat.
10. Liberally coat your rolls with the parmesan artichoke sauce, then with a liberal amount of steak mix.
11. Top everything with basil and serve.
12. Enjoy.

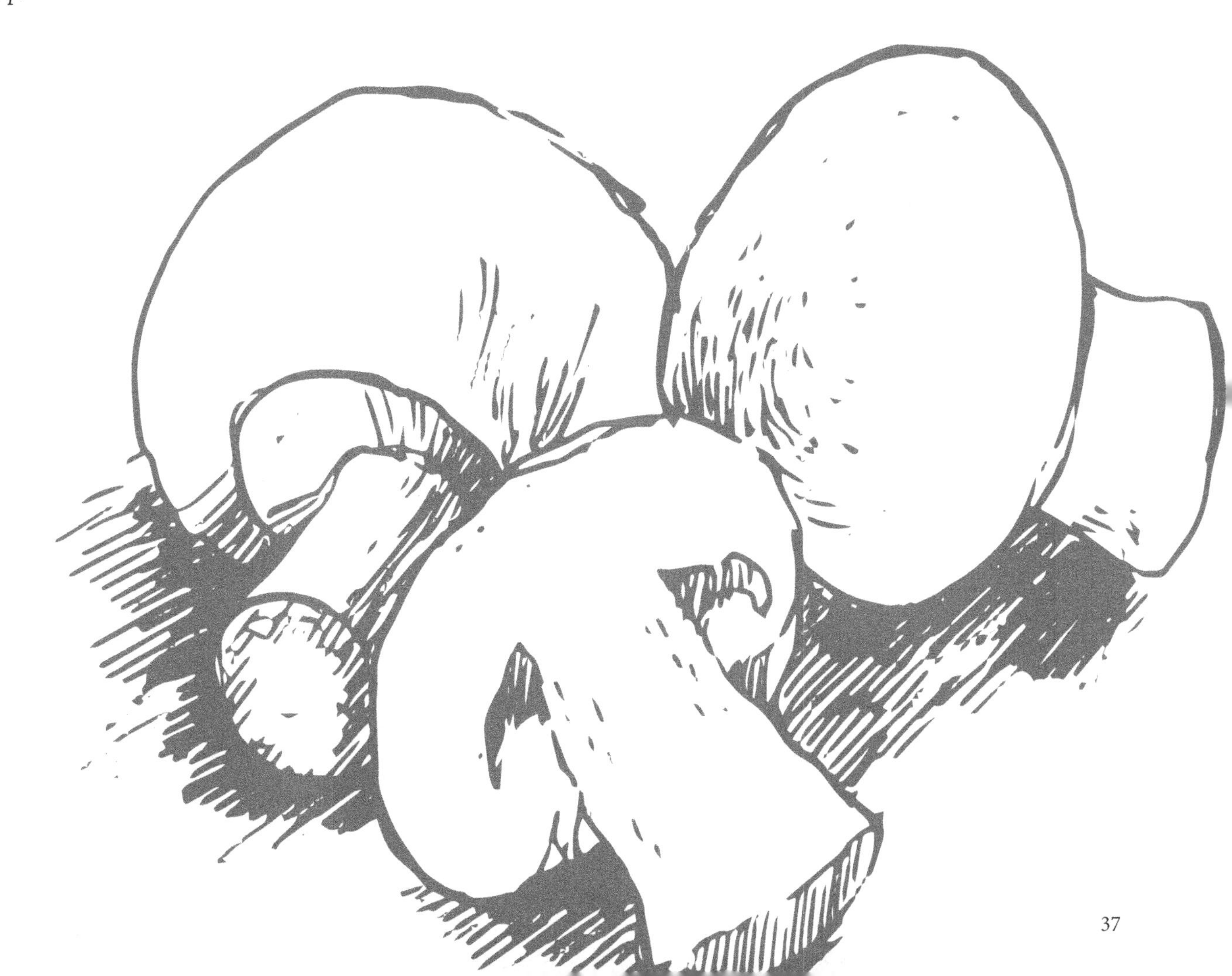

EASY RUSTIC
Apple Sandwich

Prep Time: 5 mins
Total Time: 10 mins

Servings per Recipe: 1

Calories	254 kcal
Fat	13.2 g
Carbohydrates	30.5g
Protein	4 g
Cholesterol	31 mg
Sodium	423 mg

Ingredients

1 tbsp butter
2 slices bread
3 tbsps applesauce

Directions

1. Coat 1 side of the bread with butter then place the buttered portion of the bread facing downwards in a hot frying pan.
2. Coat the top of the bread with your applesauce evenly and cook the bread for 6 mins after forming a sandwich between the two pieces.
3. Enjoy.

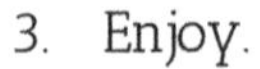

Pepper Beef Sandwich

Prep Time: 20 mins
 Total Time: 7 hrs 20 mins

Servings per Recipe: 5	
Calories	934 kcal
Fat	61.1 g
Carbohydrates	2.5g
Protein	< 87.9 g
Cholesterol	1295 mg
Sodium	4110 mg

Ingredients

5 lbs chuck roast
2 cubes beef bouillon
2 tbsps salt
2 tsps garlic salt
2 bay leaves
2 tbsps whole black peppercorns
2 tsps dried oregano
1 1/2 tsps dried rosemary

Directions

1. Submerge your chuck in water.
2. Add in the garlic salt, regular salt and bouillon.
3. Stir in the spices evenly then add the following to a coffee filter: rosemary, bay leaves, oregano, and peppercorns.
4. Seal the spices in the filter with a rubber band and place the bundle into the water with the chuck.
5. Get everything boiling, set the heat to low, place a lid on the pot, and let the chuck cook for 7 hrs.
6. Throw away the bundle of spices and place the meat to the side to lose some of heat.
7. After the chuck has cooled shred it into pieces and serve the meat on toasted rolls.
8. When serving your chuck top the meat liberally with the broth.
9. Enjoy.

PEANUT and Olive Sandwich

Prep Time: 10 mins
Total Time: 10 mins

Servings per Recipe: 1

Calories	360 kcal
Fat	22 g
Carbohydrates	32.1g
Protein	12.4 g
Cholesterol	0 mg
Sodium	1239 mg

Ingredients

2 tbsps peanut butter
2 slices bread
8 green olives, sliced

Directions

1. Coat 1 piece of bread with peanut butter then evenly with your olives.
2. Form a sandwich with the other piece of bread.
3. Enjoy.

Beef Broiled Sandwich

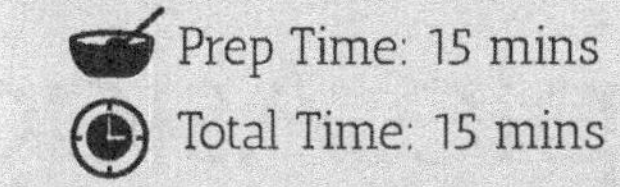Prep Time: 15 mins
Total Time: 15 mins

Servings per Recipe: 4	
Calories	228 kcal
Fat	17.8 g
Carbohydrates	3.4g
Protein	13.2 g
Cholesterol	46 mg
Sodium	261 mg

Ingredients

1 C. chopped cooked beef
2 stalks celery, chopped
1 carrot, diced
1/4 C. chopped onion
3 tbsps mayonnaise
1/4 tsp salt
1/8 tsp ground black pepper
1/8 tsp garlic powder
2 sesame seed buns, toasted until the broiler

Directions

1. Get a bowl, combine: garlic powder, beef, black pepper, celery, salt, carrot, mayo, and onion. Stir the mix until it is even.
2. Enjoy on toasted sesame seed buns.

TANDOORI
Apple Asiago Sandwich

Prep Time: 15 mins
Total Time: 30 mins

Servings per Recipe: 3	
Calories	342 kcal
Fat	21.9 g
Carbohydrates	30.5g
Protein	9.5 g
Cholesterol	26 mg
Sodium	492 mg

Ingredients

1 apple, cored and chopped
1/3 bunch kale, chopped
1 tbsp tandoori seasoning
1 tsp cayenne pepper
1/4 C. apple cider
1 tbsp olive oil
4 slices turkey bacon
3 large cracked wheat dinner-style rolls, split
3 tbsps grated Asiago cheese

Directions

1. Fry your bacon for 11 mins then place the bacon on some paper towel to drain.
2. Begin to stir the following in the apple cider, apples, cayenne, kale, and tandoori spice.
3. Top the mix with the olive oil as it fries in the bacon fat and let everything cook for 8 mins. Then place the mix to the side.
4. Evenly coat the bottom piece of the bread with the tandoori mix then with some bacon and asiago.
5. Form sandwiches with the other half of the bread.
6. Enjoy.

Crab Salad Sandwich

Prep Time: 15 mins
Total Time: 50 mins

Servings per Recipe: 2	
Calories	478 kcal
Fat	30 g
Carbohydrates	39.7g
Protein	13 g
Cholesterol	48 mg
Sodium	1413 mg

Ingredients

1 (8 oz.) package imitation crab or lobster meat
1/4 C. mayonnaise
1 tbsp finely chopped red onion
1 tsp lemon juice
1/4 tsp seafood Seasoning
1 tbsp butter, softened
2 hot dog buns

Directions

1. Get a bowl, combine: seafood seasoning, crab (flaked), lemon juice, mayo, and onions.
2. Place a covering of plastic around the bowl and put everything in the oven for 35 mins.
3. Now get your oven's broiler hot before continuing
4. Place your buns in a broiler pan after coating them with the butter.
5. Broil the bread until it is nicely toasted for a few mins then top each one evenly with the crab salad.
6. Enjoy.

TUNA
Sandwich Done Right

Prep Time: 15 mins
Total Time: 15 mins

Servings per Recipe: 2

Calories	553 kcal
Fat	32.9 g
Carbohydrates	30.2g
Protein	33.7 g
Cholesterol	63 mg
Sodium	656 mg

Ingredients

1 (6 oz.) can tuna, drained
1/4 C. mayonnaise
1 1/2 tsps cream-style horseradish sauce
1 tbsp chopped dill pickles
2 leaves lettuce
2 slices Swiss cheese
4 slices bread
2 slices tomato
2 thin slices red onion

Directions

1. Get a bowl, combine: pickles, tuna, horseradish, and mayo. Stir the mix until it even and smooth.
2. Top 2 pieces of bread with 1 piece of Swiss and a piece of lettuce. Evenly divide your tuna mix between the bread slices then layer your onions and tomatoes.
3. Place the other piece of bread to make a sandwich.
4. Enjoy.

Hawaiian Pineapple Fish Sandwich

Prep Time: 10 mins
Total Time: 25 mins

Servings per Recipe: 4	
Calories	369 kcal
Fat	16 g
Carbohydrates	32.5g
Protein	23 g
Cholesterol	41 mg
Sodium	613 mg

Ingredients

4 hamburger buns, split
2 tbsps butter
1 (6 oz.) can tuna chunks in olive oil
1 tbsp lemon juice
salt and freshly ground black pepper to taste
1 dash chili powder
1 C. shredded lettuce
1 C. shredded mozzarella cheese
4 canned pineapple rings

Directions

1. Set your oven to 350 degrees before doing anything else.
2. Toast the buns under the broiler then coat the insides with some butter.
3. Remove 1/2 of the oil from your cans of tuna then place the tuna in a bowl with: chili powder, lemon juice, pepper, and salt.
4. Stir the mix to evenly distribute the spices then divide the mix between your toasted buns.
5. Now place the following on top: 1 piece of pineapple, some lettuce, and mozzarella.
6. Form the sandwiches and place them on a cookie sheet.
7. Put the sandwiches in the oven for 11 mins or until you find the cheese has melted.
8. Enjoy.

SOY

Sandwich (Vegetarian Approved)

Prep Time: 15 mins
Total Time: 45 mins

Servings per Recipe: 4	
Calories	622 kcal
Fat	41.6 g
Carbohydrates	43.7g
Protein	21.4 g
Cholesterol	11 mg
Sodium	1332 mg

Ingredients

1 (12 oz.) package firm tofu - drained, patted dry, and sliced into 4 slices
1 C. bread crumbs
1 tsp kelp powder
1/4 tsp garlic powder
1/4 tsp paprika
1/4 tsp onion powder or flakes
1 tsp salt
olive oil, as needed
Tartar Sauce
1/2 C. mayonnaise
1/4 C. dill pickle relish
1 tbsp fresh lemon juice
4 whole wheat hamburger buns, split

Directions

1. Set your oven to 350 degrees before doing anything else.
2. Get a bowl, combine: salt, bread crumbs, onion powder, kelp powder, paprika, and garlic powder.
3. Coat your pieces of tofu with some olive oil then dredge them in the dry mix.
4. Lay the tofu in a jellyroll pan and cook them in the oven for 35 mins.
5. Watch the tofu and flip the pieces once the top side is browned.
6. At the same time get a bowl and combine: lemon juice, mayo, and relish. Stir the mix until it is smooth.
7. When about 5 mins of baking time is left. Coat the tofu with some olive oil and continue cooking everything.
8. When eating your tofu dip the pieces in the relish mix.
9. Enjoy.

Ranch Style
Cod Sandwich

Prep Time: 10 mins
Total Time: 30 mins

Servings per Recipe: 4	
Calories	313 kcal
Fat	12.6 g
Carbohydrates	26.3g
Protein	24.1 g
Cholesterol	58 mg
Sodium	537 mg

Ingredients

1 lb cod fillets
1 clove garlic, minced
1 lemon, cut into wedges
2 tbsps butter, softened
1 pinch salt and ground black pepper to taste
2 tbsps steak sauce
4 hamburger buns, split and toasted
2 tbsps Ranch-style salad dressing

Directions

1. Set your oven to 350 degrees before doing anything else.
2. Lay your pieces of fish in a jellyroll pan and top them with: lemon juice, and garlic.
3. Now dot everything with the butter evenly and cook the fish in the oven for 22 mins.
4. Coat the bottom of your pieces of bread with the steak sauce then lay a piece of fish over the sauce.
5. Top the fish with ranch and form a sandwich with the other piece of bread.
6. Enjoy.

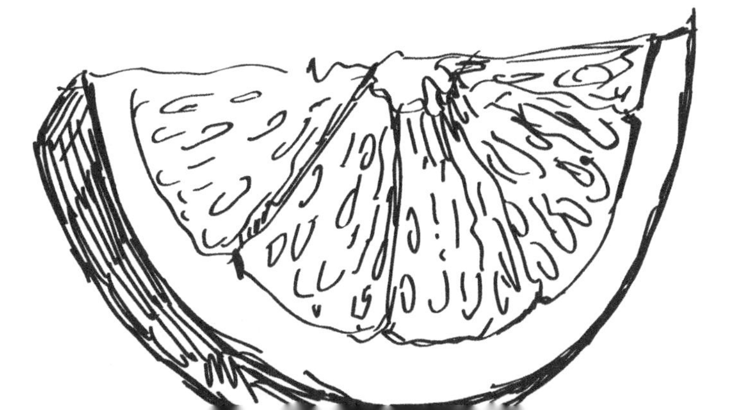

PARMIGIANO-REGGIANO Sandwich

Prep Time: 10 mins
Total Time: 16 mins

Servings per Recipe: 4	
Calories	748 kcal
Fat	50.1 g
Carbohydrates	30.4g
Protein	43 g
Cholesterol	135 mg
Sodium	2211 mg

Ingredients

1/4 C. butter, softened
1 C. freshly grated Parmigiano-Reggiano cheese
8 slices cooked turkey bacon
4 slices Cheddar cheese
8 slices sourdough bread

Directions

1. Get a bowl, evenly mix: parmesan, and butter.
2. Get a frying hot with nonstick spray.
3. Layer one piece of cheddar, and two pieces of bacon on half of your pieces of bread. Then put another piece of bread to form a sandwich. Coat sandwich with butter parmesan mix on both sides.
4. Cook for 4 mins per side.
5. Enjoy.

A Texas Cajun Egg Sandwich Breakfast

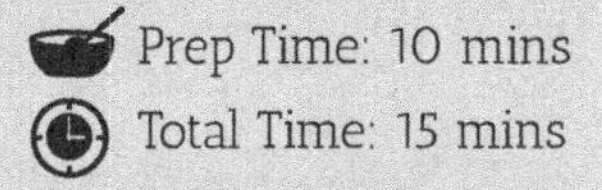

Servings per Recipe: 1	
Calories	471 kcal
Fat	31.5 g
Carbohydrates	29.6g
Protein	18.1 g
Cholesterol	248 mg
Sodium	996 mg

Ingredients

1 tbsp butter
1 egg
1 slice Cheddar cheese
1 tsp mayonnaise, or to taste
1 tsp mustard, or to taste
1 tsp ketchup, or to taste
1 pinch Cajun seasoning, or to taste
1 dash hot pepper sauce (such as Tabasco(R))
2 slices white bread, toasted
1 lettuce leaf
1 slice tomato

Directions

1. Fry your egg for 3 mins in butter then flip it.
2. Top the egg with the cheese and cook everything until the cheese melts for about 3 more mins. Then add your Cajun seasoning.
3. Coat both your bread pieces with: ketchup, mustard, and mayo.
4. Layer a piece of tomato and some lettuce on a piece of bread then put the egg on top and add some hot sauce.
5. Add a bit more Cajun spice and add the other piece of bread to from a sandwich.
6. Enjoy.

Made in the USA
Las Vegas, NV
05 October 2021

31737256R00031